THIS BOOK BELONGS TO MY FAVORITE
MILLENNIAL MOMMY:

_____

MY MOMMY'S A MILLENNIAL

Written by Meredith Vivian & Hugo Maldonado
Editorial development and Illustrations produced by Hugo Maldonado
Cover design and Illustrations by Anissa Sia

This book is dedicated to all the
millennial super moms!

Hi! My name's Marleigh and my mommy's a millennial.

What exactly does it mean to be a millennial? Let me tell you!

Well, for starters, my mommy loves to take pictures of me for her Instagram!

She made me my own Instagram even though I can't read
and I don't have a phone!

My mommy only feeds me organic and gluten free foods.

Grandpa and Grandma always tell her
"but you ate whatever you wanted and
turned out just fine!"

She huffs and calls them
"boomers."

I'm pretty sure my mommy is in love with someone named Amazon Prime.

He shows up every single day to drop
off new clothes for her.

My mommy loves to wear the same outfits as me... even though she's 35 and I'm 2.

Because we're "twinning!"

My mommy is constantly filming me for her Snapchat.

I feel like a movie star being stalked by paparazzi.

My mommy is a Capricorn.

She says we only get along
because I'm a Taurus and
our signs are compatible.

My mommy really wants to buy us a house.

But she can't because of her crippling student loan debt and her addiction to avocado toast.

My mommy's a crazy millennial.

But she's the perfect mommy for me!

CPSIA information can be obtained
at www.ICGtesting.com
Printed in the USA
LVHW021246131021
700314LV00015B/1057

9 781087 988207